GRAPHIC CAREERS
SECRET AGENTS

by Gary Jeffrey

illustrated by Terry Riley

New York

Published in 2008 by The Rosen Publishing Group, Inc.
29 East 21st Street, New York, NY 10010

Copyright © 2008 David West Books

First edition, 2008

Designed and produced by
David West Books

Editor: Gail Bushnell

Photo credits:
P5t, Library of Congress; 6t, National Archives; 6m, Tagishsimon, 6bl, Philippe Kurlapski, 6br, Andrzej Barabasz; 7tr, Matt Crypto, 7tl, National Security Agency, 7m, Image courtesy of the 30th Space Wing, 7b, www.fema.gov

  Library of Congress Cataloging-in-Publication Data

Jeffrey, Gary.
  Secret agents / Gary Jeffrey. -- 1st ed.
     p. cm. -- (Graphic careers)
  Includes index.
  ISBN 978-1-4042-1464-4 (library binding) -- ISBN 978-1-4042-1465-1
(pbk.) -- ISBN 978-1-4042-1466-8 (6 pack)
 1. Spies. 2. Espionage--Vocational guidance. 3. Intelligence
service--United States. I. Title.
  UB270.J44 2008
  327.12730023--dc22
                                              2007043334

CONTENTS

ESPIONAGE

A secret agent is a spy—someone paid to get secrets. Modern-day spies who work for governments are called "intelligence officers," but the practice of spying is as old as civilization itself.

SPYMASTERS

As far back as ancient China, people have used spying to gain an advantage over their enemies. Monarchs relied on domestic espionage to keep them in power. George Washington ran an amazingly successful spy ring against the

Francis Walsingham, spymaster to Queen Elizabeth I, discovered and disarmed two plots to overthrow her.

British during the Revolutionary War. His agents' information told him when to fight and when to flee. In wartime, a well-run secret service can make the difference between victory and defeat.

DOUBLE AGENTS

Double agents are spies who secretly work against their own employer for the enemy. "Doubles" are often captured agents who have been threatened with punishment unless they "turn." By using double agents, the British Secret Service captured every German sent to spy in World War II.

A British criminal, trained to be a spy by the Nazis, Agent Zig Zag, Eddie Chapman, was one of many operatives used by the British in their Double Cross system.

THE COST OF SPYING

Spying can be exciting and important work, but it's not without risk. Espionage is considered an act of treason in many countries, and captured spies could often expect to pay the ultimate price. In 1780 the head of British Secret Intelligence, Major John Andre, was hanged by the American revolutionaries. He had been found in disguise, carrying plans of attack written by the turncoat Benedict Arnold.

Engraving showing the capture of John Andre.

Rose O'Neal Greenhow, was imprisoned in the Capitol in 1861 for passing Union Battle plans to the Confederates. Her spying helped the rebels to victory at the first battle of Bull Run.

TO MAKE A SPY

Successful spies are usually recruited by an intelligence officer because they have direct access to sensitive information. Others are used as go-betweens to ferry secrets.

Agents need to work in jobs that offer a good "cover story." Being a diplomat, traveling salesman, or an academic is useful if you intend to spy for a living.

Great spies have three key features—intelligence, bravery, and a natural ability to hide who they really are.

Richard Sorge, seen here on a Russian postage stamp, is widely regarded as the most impressive spy ever. Post World War I, German war hero Sorge became a spy for the Soviets. In 1934, he set up a spy ring in Japan (they had recently invaded north China). During WWII he warned Stalin about Germany's invasion of Russia, and in 1941 found out that Japan intended to attack the Allies, thus enabling the release of Russia's eastern troops for the defense of Moscow. Sorge was executed by the Japanese in 1944.

American S. G. Morley was an archaeologist. He used his job to spy on the Germans in World War I.

THE SPYING GAME

The Office of Strategic Services (OSS), America's highly effective World War II intelligence agency, was the brainchild of veteran soldier William J. Donovan. When the OSS was broken up after the war, he called President Truman with a new idea.

In 1941, "Wild" Bill Donovan became the first overall chief of U.S. intelligence.

COMPANY BUSINESS

The proposal was for a Central Intelligence Agency (CIA) similar to the British Secret Intelligence Service (MI6). The CIA would gather information by both overt and covert means, and collect together material from all other government agencies. Through the postwar years, pitted against the ruthless Soviet intelligence machine called the KGB, the "company" expanded rapidly.

The seal of the CIA.

The U.S. government today runs sixteen separate agencies that use the latest technology, but the most basic source of intelligence hasn't changed—people.

MI6 headquarters, London, United Kingdom.

HUMINT

HUMan INTelligence is material gained from human contact. It might be offered by a defector or a paid informant, (often with a dubious background). Or it might be extracted by interrogating a prisoner or forwarded by a mole (or planted covert operator). The collection of effective HUMINT can be a dirty and dangerous business.

In the cold war, agents used miniature cameras to photograph secret documents. Today, memory sticks are used to pass computerized data to interested parties.

SIGINT

From the legendary code-breaking machines of World War II to postwar telephone tapping, SIGnals INTelligence agencies have intercepted secret messages. In America, SIGINT is handled by the National Security Agency, where massed teams of cryptanalysts monitor global radio, telephone, and Internet communications.

An NSA "listening" antenna in the United Kingdom.

NSA headquarters in Maryland. It is thought that more than 30,000 people staff this facility alone.

IMINT

IMagery INTelligence is material gathered from aerial and satellite photographs. Modern technology enables agencies like the U.S. National Reconnaisance Office (NRO) to study the ground in incredible detail. However, IMINT alone cannot tell you what an enemy might be thinking ... or planning.

(Inset) The Pentagon, pictured in 1962 by the first U.S. spy satellite, Corona. (Main image) The 2005 launch of an NRO satellite.

21ST-CENTURY THREATS

The rise of terrorism is a huge concern to the democratic nations of the world. Far from being outmoded, the secret agent is needed now more than ever, to infiltrate and get information—to *spy*.

Might the information from well placed secret agents have prevented 9/11 from happening?

WULF SCHMIDT
AGENT A3725
SUPERSPY

SEPTEMBER 19, 1940. A BLACK-PAINTED HEINKEL AIRCRAFT FLIES LOW OVER THE CAMBRIDGESHIRE COUNTRYSIDE IN ENGLAND. INSIDE, IT CARRIES A LONE PARATROOPER—WULF SCHMIDT, A GERMAN AGENT TRAINED BY THE ABWEHR*...

GET READY. IT'S ALMOST

THIS IS GOING TO GO WRONG—I CAN FEEL IT!

*GERMAN MILITARY INTELLIGENCE.

A SUDDEN GUST ROCKS THE AIRPLANE.

AAAAAGH—MY HAND!

NNAAAAAAAAAAAAAAAAAAAAAAGH!

AFTER BURYING HIS 'CHUTE, HE HEADS FOR THE NEAREST TOWN.

ACH, MY WRIST IS SO SORE...

NNNGH...THAT'S BETTER.

...NEED TO SLEEP...

BLINK!

THE LOCALS HAVE BEEN WARNED TO LOOK OUT FOR STRANGERS.

I THINK THE HOME DEFENSE NEEDS TO KNOW ABOUT THIS.

SCHMIDT BUYS A NEW WATCH BUT IS UNSURE HOW MUCH BRITISH MONEY TO GIVE...

THANK YOU. ER... CAN YOU HELP ME WITH THE CURRENCY, PLEASE?

EXCUSE ME, SIR, I THINK YOU NEED TO COME WITH US.

HE IS HANDED OVER TO MI5*...

CAMP 020?

MP 20

*THE BRITISH SECURITY SERVICE.

THIS IS IT. I'M GOING TO BE **SHOT!**

020, AKA, LATCHMERE HOUSE, IN SURREY, RUN BY MI5.

WELCOME, "HARRY WILLIAMSON"...OR SHOULD I SAY AGENT A3725? OH, AND WE KNOW EXACTLY WHY YOU'RE HERE.

YOU'VE COME TO GATHER INTELLIGENCE ON OUR HOME DEFENSES FOR A GERMAN *INVASION.*

YES, YES—BUT *HOW* DO THEY KNOW?

NINE MONTHS EARLIER, BLETCHLEY PARK, BUCKINGHAMSHIRE, ENGLAND...

I'VE FOUND OUT WHICH BOOK THEY'RE USING!

HUGH TREVOR-ROPER IS AN OPERATIVE FOR MI8.*

*SIGNALS INTELLIGENCE.

EXCELLENT WORK ROPER, IT'S THE BREAKTHROUGH WE'VE BEEN LOOKING FOR!

FOR MONTHS TREVOR-ROPER HAD BEEN ANALYZING GERMAN FIELD AGENTS' RADIO COMMUNICATIONS.

HE HAD FIGURED OUT THAT THEY WERE USING A BOOK CODE.

441012
page 44
line 10
word 12

THE SYSTEM USED NUMBERS TO IDENTIFY WHERE MESSAGE WORDS COULD BE FOUND IN DUPLICATE READING BOOKS.

NOW WE'LL GET ADVANCE WARNING OF WHEN AND WHERE THEIR AGENTS ARE ARRIVING.

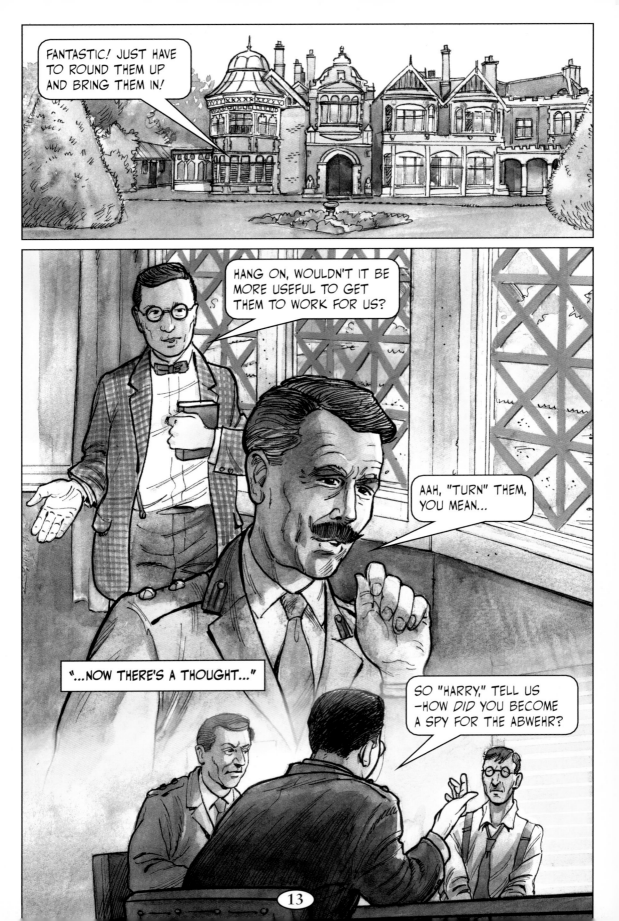

LATER...

WELL, WHAT DO YOU THINK?

HMM...A DANISH GERMAN WITH A LUST FOR ADVENTURE, AND NO FIRM POLITICAL BELIEFS...

...HE'S PERFECT.

SCHMIDT READILY AGREES TO BECOME A DOUBLE AGENT. HIS NEW CODE NAME IS *TATE*...

BECAUSE YOU LOOK LIKE HARRY TATE, THE MUSIC HALL STAR. HEH HEH!

HIS FIELD RADIO HAS BEEN RETURNED.

RIGHT, STATIONS, EVERYBODY— WE'VE GOT TWO MINUTES!

SCHMIDT HAS BEEN GROOMED BY HIS MI5 HANDLER, THOMAS ROBERTSON, TO MAKE HIS FIRST BROADCAST HOME.

CLICK-CLICK-CLICK-CLICK...

"THIS IS A3725, CALLING HAMBURG."

DOT-DOT-DOT-DASH-DASH-DOT...

"HAMBURG RECEIVING. WHAT IS YOUR STATUS, A3725?"

YES!

SCHMIDT SENDS A CAREFULLY PREPARED MIXTURE OF REAL AND FALSE INFORMATION TO THE ABWEHR STATION.

CLICK...CLICK...CLICK-CLICK...

A RADIO OPERATOR STANDS BY WHO HAS LEARNED HOW TO DUPLICATE HIS "FIST"* IN CASE HE NEEDS TO BE RELIEVED.

*PARTICULAR WAY OF TAPPING MORSE.

GOOD JOB! WE'LL JUST HAVE TO SEE HOW IT TRICKLES DOWN.

WHEN THE NAZI V1 AND V2 TERROR ROCKETS COME TO LONDON, HE TRANSMITS FALSE COORDINATES FOR THEIR IMPACTS, INDICATING THEY HAD OVERSHOT THEIR TARGETS.

KAABOOOM!

THE ROCKETS ARE RECALIBRATED, CAUSING MANY TO FALL SHORT.

NEAR THE END OF THE WAR...

CAN YOU BELIEVE IT? THE NAZIS HAVE GIVEN HIM A PAY BONUS!

IT'S AS IF THEY CAN'T ALLOW THEMSELVES TO BELIEVE HE MIGHT BE FAKE.

SCHMIDT WAS ALSO AWARDED THE GERMAN IRON CROSS, BUT NEVER COLLECTED IT, PREFERRING TO RETIRE AT THE WAR'S END TO A QUIET LIFE AS A BRITISH CITIZEN.

CODENAME TATE

THE MEDAL IS CURRENTLY DISPLAYED *SOMEWHERE* IN MI5 HEADQUARTERS.

THE END

17

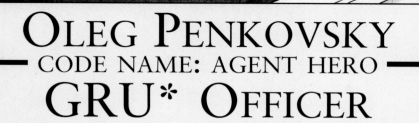

OLEG PENKOVSKY
— CODE NAME: AGENT HERO —
GRU* OFFICER

EARLY APRIL 1961, 11 GORKY STREET, MOSCOW, RUSSIA. GREVILLE WYNNE, A BRITISH BUSINESSMAN, IS ORGANIZING A BRITISH VISIT FOR SOME RUSSIAN BUSINESSMEN WITH COLONEL OLEG PENKOVSKY...

*SOVIET MILITARY INTELLIGENCE AGENCY.

...AND HERE IS A LIST OF THE MEN WHO WILL BE COMING.

BUT I DON'T UNDERSTAND, OLEG— YOUR NAME IS AT THE TOP.

YES. I MUST COME TO LONDON, BUT NOT FOR PLEASURE. I...

...I HAVE THINGS TO *TELL* YOU.

WYNNE IS NOT TAKEN ABACK. IN FACT, HE KNOWS WHAT TO DO, BECAUSE GREVILLE WYNNE IS *A BRITISH SPY.*

LATER, WHEN WYNNE EXAMINES THE CONTENTS OF THE PACKAGE, HE FINDS...

MY WORD, OLEG'S INTELLIGENCE IS GOLD, PURE GOLD!

APRIL 21, MOUNT ROYAL HOTEL, LONDON.

WELL, HE SEEMS TO BE THE REAL DEAL...

...ON PAPER, AT LEAST.

KNOCK KNOCK

THAT'LL BE HIM.

JOE BULIK IS THE CIA'S HEAD OF COVERT OPERATIONS, MOSCOW STATION.

HAROLD SHERGOLD AND MIKE STOKES ARE BRITISH MI6 OFFICERS. ALSO PRESENT IS U.S. RUSSIAN INTERPRETER GEORGE KISEVALTER.

THIS IS INTERESTING INFORMATION, COLONEL PENKOVSKY—BUT WHY?

WHY AM I DOING THIS?

YES.

FOR WORLD PEACE. MY LEADER, KHRUSHCHEV IS, IN MY OPINION, A MADMAN AND A CROOK.

ALSO, HE DOES NOT RESPECT THE ARMY.

HE HAS CHEATED THE WAR VETERANS OUT OF THEIR PENSIONS, AMONG MANY OTHER CRIMES...

HIS INFORMATION IS DYNAMITE, BULIK. BUT CAN WE TRUST HIM?

BACK AT CIA HEADQUARTERS IN VIRGINIA, BULIK TALKS TO HIS BOSS, ALLEN DULLES, ABOUT PENKOVSKY'S POTENTIAL...

SIR, I'VE SEEN THE KIND OF SCAMS THE KGB* HAS TRIED ON US. I THINK PENKOVSKY IS THE GENUINE ARTICLE.

*SOVIET STATE SECURITY.

UP TO THREE HUNDRED SHOTS IN EACH MINIATURE CARTRIDGE. WHEN YOU'RE FINISHED, JUST FLIP IT OUT LIKE THIS...

"...AND REMEMBER, OLEG, WE ONLY WANT THE MOST TOP-SECRET

I AM GOING TO BE THE BEST SPY IN HISTORY!

THE FILM CANISTERS ARE LEFT AT PREARRANGED DROP-OFF SITES AROUND THE CITY...

BACK IN MOSCOW, PENKOVSKY PHOTOGRAPHS HUNDREDS OF CLASSIFIED ARMY DOCUMENTS.

...TO BE COLLECTED BY GREVILLE WYNNE.

CAPITOL HILL, WASHINGTON, D.C.

WE'VE NEVER SEEN ANYTHING LIKE IT. EACH DELIVERY IS A TREASURE TROVE OF INFORMATION!

HE'S CERTAINLY EXPOSED THE MYTH OF "THE MISSILE GAP."*

DULLES HAS BEEN MEETING WITH DEFENSE SECRETARY ROBERT MCNAMARA.

*PRESIDENT KENNEDY'S ADMINISTRATION THOUGHT THE SOVIETS HAD BETTER TECHNOLOGY AND MORE MISSILES.

IT'S LIKE WE'VE BEEN PLAYING POKER AGAINST MR. KHRUSHCHEV, AND NOW WE'VE FINALLY GOTTEN A LOOK AT HIS CARDS!

LONDON, MIDSUMMER. GREVILLE WYNNE BRIEFS PENKOVSKY ABOUT AN ALTERNATIVE CONTACT...

...HER NAME IS JANET CHISHOLM, WIFE OF AN EMBASSY OFFICIAL.

OCTOBER 22, 1962. AFTER WEEKS OF SURVEILLANCE A KGB ARREST TEAM FINALLY COMES FOR OLEG PENKOVSKY.

BY OCTOBER 28, THE CUBAN MISSILE CRISIS IS RESOLVED IN THE U.S.A.'S FAVOR. MEANWHILE, DEEP INSIDE THE LUBYANKA*...

NO, NO. YOU MUST STAY ON YOUR FEET, OLEG...

*KGB HEADQUARTERS.

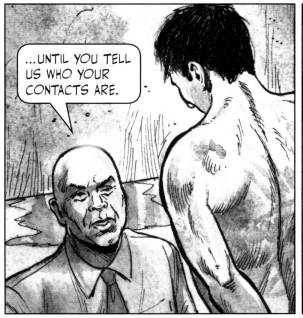

...UNTIL YOU TELL US WHO YOUR CONTACTS ARE.

NOVEMBER 2, TRADE FAIR CAMPSITE, BUDAPEST, HUNGARY.

...YES, IT WAS A GOOD NIGHT. SEE YOU TOMORROW!

29

ROBERT BAER

— CASE OFFICER —

CIA

A CALIFORNIAN BORN IN 1952, BAER SPENT HIS EARLY YEARS TRAVELING AROUND EUROPE WITH HIS MOTHER. LATER HE ATTENDED MILITARY SCHOOL AND GEORGETOWN UNIVERSITY SCHOOL OF FOREIGN SERVICE, GRADUATING IN 1975.

AUGUST 1979, NEW DELHI, INDIA.

GLAD THE MONSOON HAS FINALLY EASED OFF.

BAER, A CIA FIELD OFFICER, IS ON HIS WAY TO MEET ONE OF HIS FIVE FOREIGN AGENTS.

A LOT OF TRAFFIC. HALF THE CITY MUST BE FLOODED, SO I'LL GET HIS INFORMATION, PAY HIM, AND GET BACK ASAP.

ONE OF THE WORLD'S BIGGEST BUYERS OF SOVIET WEAPONRY, INDIA IS A HOTBED OF INTERNATIONAL ESPIONAGE.

...AND STAY SHARP, BAER, THE IB* WILL BE OUT IN FORCE TONIGHT.

*INTELLIGENCE BUREAU—INDIA'S FORMIDABLE SECRET SERVICE.

BUT HE FELT CONFIDENT. AFTER ALL, HE WAS BECOMING AN EXPERT AT THE GAME.

JUST TWO YEARS EARLIER, IT HAD BEEN A VERY DIFFERENT STORY...

YOU ARE HERE TO BECOME WOLVES, PREDATORS WHO CAN EXPERTLY SEPARATE A LAMB FROM THE FLOCK AND LEAD IT INTO BETRAYAL OF EVERYTHING IT HOLDS DEAR.

IN 1976 BAER HAD BEEN JUST ANOTHER RAW RECRUIT AT THE CIA TRAINING CENTER IN VIRGINIA CALLED "THE FARM."

...AND ALL WITHOUT GETTING CAUGHT.

JOE LYNCH WAS THE COURSE COORDINATOR.

THE TRAINEES WERE TAUGHT HOW TO SPOT POTENTIAL AGENTS...

...OFTEN FOREIGNERS WITH ACCESS TO AREAS WHERE WE CAN'T GO.

NEXT, WE **ASSESS** THEM.

DO THEY HAVE MONEY PROBLEMS? ARE THEY DISILLUSIONED WITH THEIR GOVERNMENT? FIND THE WEAK SPOT...

...THEN MAKE YOUR PITCH.

THEY WERE TAUGHT TO AVOID SURVEILLANCE...

THE TEAMS AGAINST YOU WILL USE DOLPHIN SURVEILLANCE—NOW YOU SEE US, NOW YOU DON'T.

WATERFALL SURVEILLANCE—COMING STRAIGHT TOWARD YOU, RATHER THAN FOLLOWING...

SO KEEP MOVING—THERE WILL ALWAYS BE A SPLIT SECOND WHEN THEY CAN'T SEE YOU. PREPARATION IS THE KEY.

THEY DRILLED SIXTEEN HOURS A DAY FOR SIX WEEKS.

...AND THERE WAS MORE TO COME...

VERY GOOD. NOW PUT IT BACK TOGETHER, AND DO IT AGAIN, *BLINDFOLDED.*

THE FOUR-WEEK PARAMILITARY COURSE WAS THE FINAL PHASE.

THEY LEARNED DIRECTION FINDING...

...PARACHUTE JUMPING...

REMEMBER, BAER —TUCK AND ROLL!

...AND DEMOLITIONS.

CRIMP THE BLAST CAP TOO HIGH AND **BOOM!** THERE GOES YOUR HAND.

WHEN YOU'VE MASTERED THIS, WE'RE GOING TO TRY CRIMPING THEM IN **THE DARK.**

THE TRAINING ENDED WITH A SIMULATED NIGHT OPERATION IN VIRGINIA'S TIDEWATER SWAMPS...

WE'VE GOT TWELVE HOURS TO RENDEZVOUS WITH THE AGENT AND TAKE HIM TO A WAITING BOAT.

DOESN'T LOOK FAR— SHOULDN'T TAKE MORE THAN AN HOUR TO GET THERE.

THREE HOURS LATER...

AAGH, MY HANDS—YOU NEED TO TAKE OVER.

THEN THERE WAS THE SWAMP...

GHAAAA!

JUST BEFORE DAWN, THEY FIND THE AGENT, AND, AMID A SIMULATED ATTACK...

AGENT IN FIRST! AGENT IN FIRST!

...THAT'S RIGHT, PEOPLE, THERE IS NOTHING MORE IMPORTANT TO

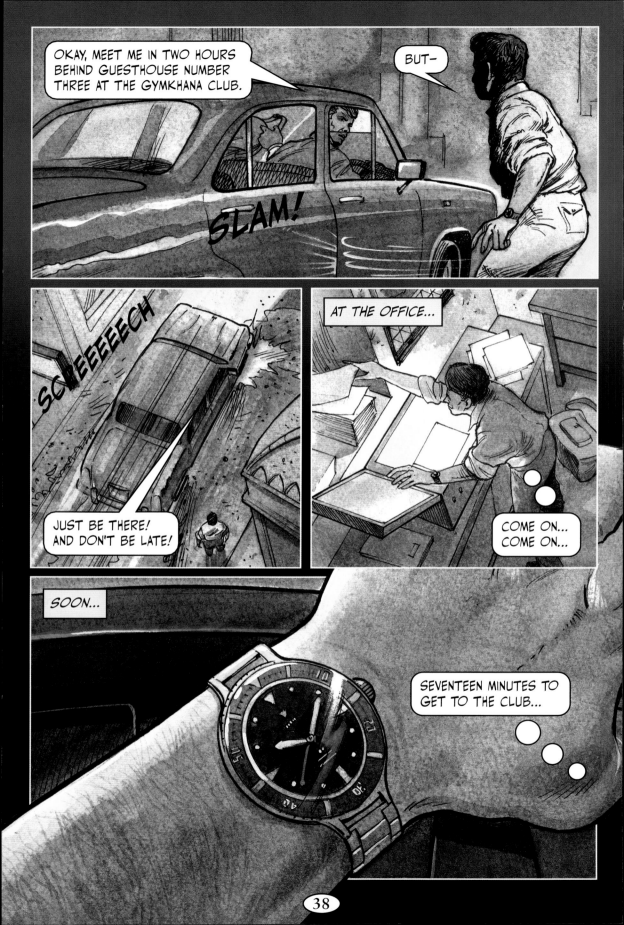

UH-OH, I'M BEING FOLLOWED.

TWO CARS—MUST BE IB. IF THEY CATCH ME, I'M FINISHED.

NO TIME TO LOSE THEM.

SIX MINUTES—ARE THEY STILL THERE? I CAN'T TELL.

SIDE ALLEY...

...FLOOR IT!

VARRROOOOOM

HUH?

WHAT THE—?!

WELL, HELLO, OLD PAL, HOW HAVE YOU BEEN?

PLEASE, STRANGER, PLAY ALONG JUST FOR A MINUTE.

?

THEY'RE GOING, PHEW! NOTHING LIKE BEATING THE ODDS...JUST BARELY!

WAITER, CAN WE GET TWO MORE COFFEES HERE? THANKS.

ROBERT BAER LATER SERVED IN BEIRUT, LEBANON, TAJIKISTAN, AND NORTHERN IRAQ. IN 1998, HE WAS AWARDED THE CAREER INTELLIGENCE MEDAL.

THE END

HOW TO BECOME A
SECRET AGENT

Getting employed to spy for your country is very difficult to accomplish. Security agencies like the CIA are only interested in the brightest and best applicants. But if you are really interested in a career as a spy, that should not deter you from going for it.

REQUIREMENTS

The CIA is divided into the Directorate of Intelligence and the Directorate of Operations. The DI analyzes and filters information gathered by the agents, or case officers, of the DO. To become a case officer you will need to be a U.S. citizen and have a bachelor's degree with a grade point average of 3.0 or above.

STEPS TO BECOMING A CIA CASE OFFICER

1. Get specialized experience. If you have military experience, are fluently multilingual, and have advanced qualifications in economics, sciences, math, psychology, or computer science, you could be just what the CIA needs.

2. Be a model citizen. If the CIA *is* interested in you, they will spy on you. A clean criminal record is essential to becoming a case officer.

3. Apply online and be patient. Check out the Clandestine Service career section on the CIA Web site, so that you can submit your résumé for a specific position. Be aware that it may take up to a year to finish the application process.

4. Research some alternative careers. Look carefully at other possibilities so that you can be sure to choose the job that will use your talents and suit you best. You could become an analyst. Other security agencies, like the NSA, are always needing to recruit intelligence and signal analysts. Although it is a desk job, this is an important role that is very much a part of the action.

Spying for your country is one of the toughest careers to follow. Fail, and you risk going to prison. Succeed, and no one can ever know of your achievements.

GLOSSARY

archaeology The study of our past through exploration, excavation, and analysis of places and items uncovered.

brief To give someone detailed information about a subject.

circulated Passed around, as information from agent to agent and country to country.

cold war After World War II, the United States and the Soviet Union engaged in a contest of spying and propaganda, which was called the "cold war."

covert Hidden, or secret.

cryptanalyst Someone who encrypts or decodes messages using a code key.

D-day landings Invasion of mainland Europe by the Allied Forces during World War II.

defector A spy who abandons his or her own country for another one.

democratic Believing in equal rights for everyone.

diplomatic Professional international relations.

double agent An agent who spies against his or her government.

encoded Changed into a coded form.

encrypted Encoded.

Enigma A machine developed during World War II which encrypted and decoded messages.

espionage The practice of using spies to gain information.

gymkhana An East Indian sports club.

handler An agent who instructs and controls subordinate agents.

infiltrate To secretly gain access to the inside of an organization.

Iron Cross A medal awarded for bravery by the German Army during World War II.

mole An agent who gains employment in a target organization and remains there, spying, for a long time.

Morse code A code in which a sequence of long and short radio signals or flashes of light represents letters or words.

operative An undercover agent.

outmoded Old-fashioned or out of date.

overt Business conducted out in the open.

potential Qualities or abilities that may be developed for future success.

resolved Settled or finalized.

treason The crime of betraying one's country.

turncoat A disloyal person who deserts his or her friends, country, or particular group.

FOR MORE INFORMATION

ORGANIZATIONS

Central Intelligence Agency (CIA)
Office of Public Affairs
Washington, D.C. 20505
(703) 482-0623
http://www.cia.gov

Secret Intelligence Service
SIS
PO Box 1300
London SE1 1BD
http://www.mi6.gov.uk

FOR FURTHER READING

Coleman, Janet Wyman. The International Spy Museum. *Secrets, Lies, Gizmos and Spies: A History of Spies and Espionage.* Washington, D.C.: Abrams Books, 2006.

International Spy Museum. *I Lie for a Living: Greatest Spies of All Time.* New York, NY: National Geographic, 2006.

Payment, Simone. *American Women Spies of World War II.* New York, NY: Rosen Publishing Group, 2004.

Wiese, Jim. *Spy Science: 40 Secret-Sleuthing, Code-Cracking, Spy-Catching Activities for Kids.* New York, NY: Rosen Publishing Group, 2004.

INDEX

Web Sites

Due to the changing nature of Internet links, Rosen Publishing has developed an online list of Web sites related to the subject of this book. This site is updated regularly. Please use this link to access the list:

http://www.rosenlinks.com/gc/seag